Woodland Mandalas

A coloring book to inspire your senses & relax your mind.

Rebecca Roelant-Wauson

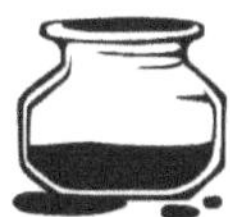

Printed in the United States of America

Graphic Design by Inkwell Book Co.
Illustrations by Rebecca Roelant-Wauson

First Edition Printing, 2016

ISBN 978-0-9972246-1-0

Inkwell Book Co.
1520 W. Main St., suite 206
Richmond, VA 23220

www.InkwellBookCompany.com
www.etsy.com/shop/wordsremember

Woodland Mandalas was conceived when I stumbled across the wonderful world of mandalas. I was attracted to their circular designs, parallel lines, attention to detail, and rich colors. Mandalas have evolved from religious symbols to art forms; in fact, mandala means "circle" or "center" and many people have used mandalas as a way to restore balance and enhance relaxation. Personally, it is the patterns and the symmetry that speak to my inner OCD tendencies; when I finish a mandala I have brought order and perfection to a small part of my world. I cherish that experience.

I decided upon a woodland theme because of our location in the mountains. We are blessed to see many of the animals and plants featured in this coloring book on a daily basis and I drew my inspiration from many of the patterns I see around me.

May these designs enrich your creative spirit and sooth your soul!

—Rebecca

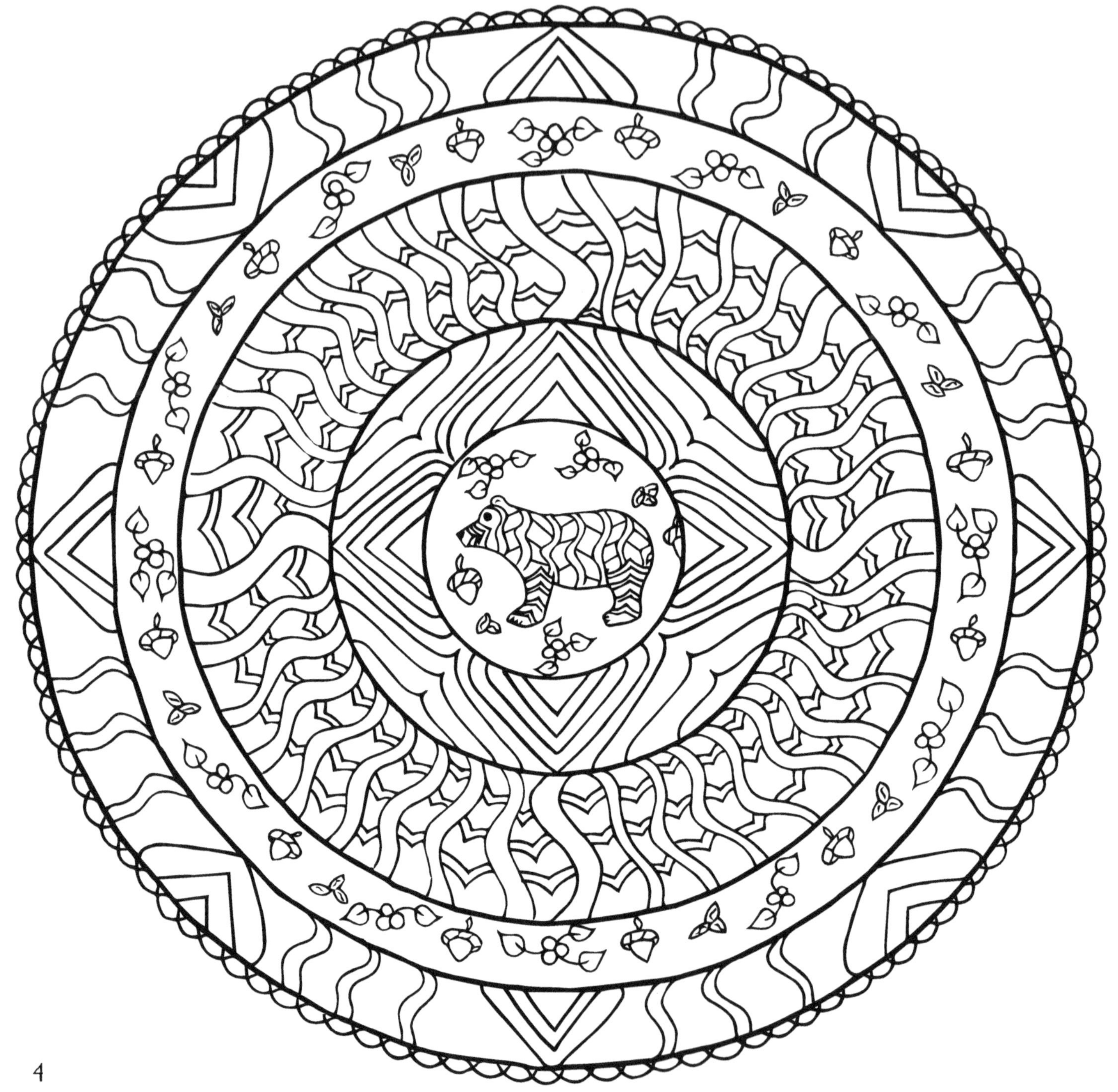

4

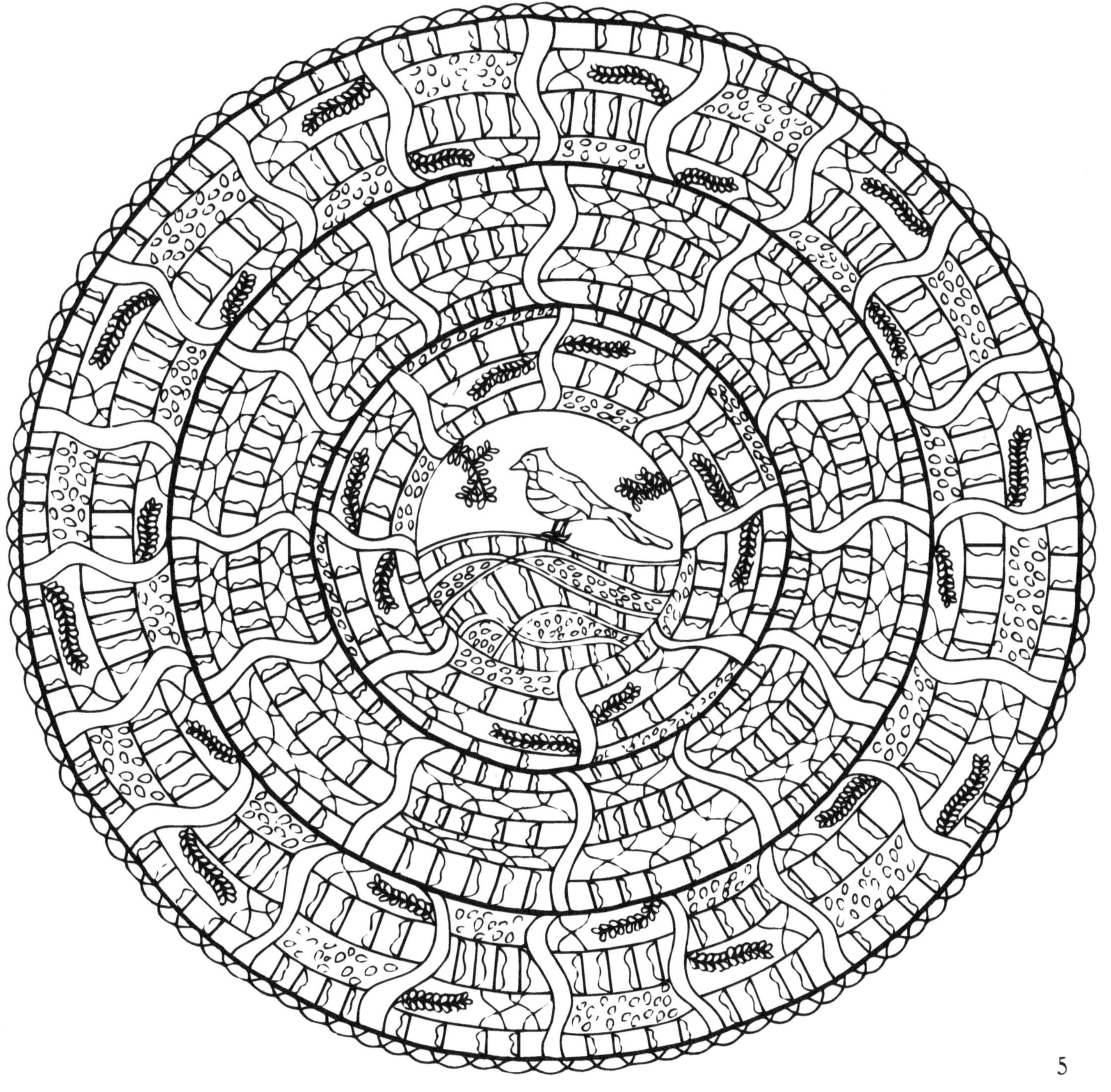

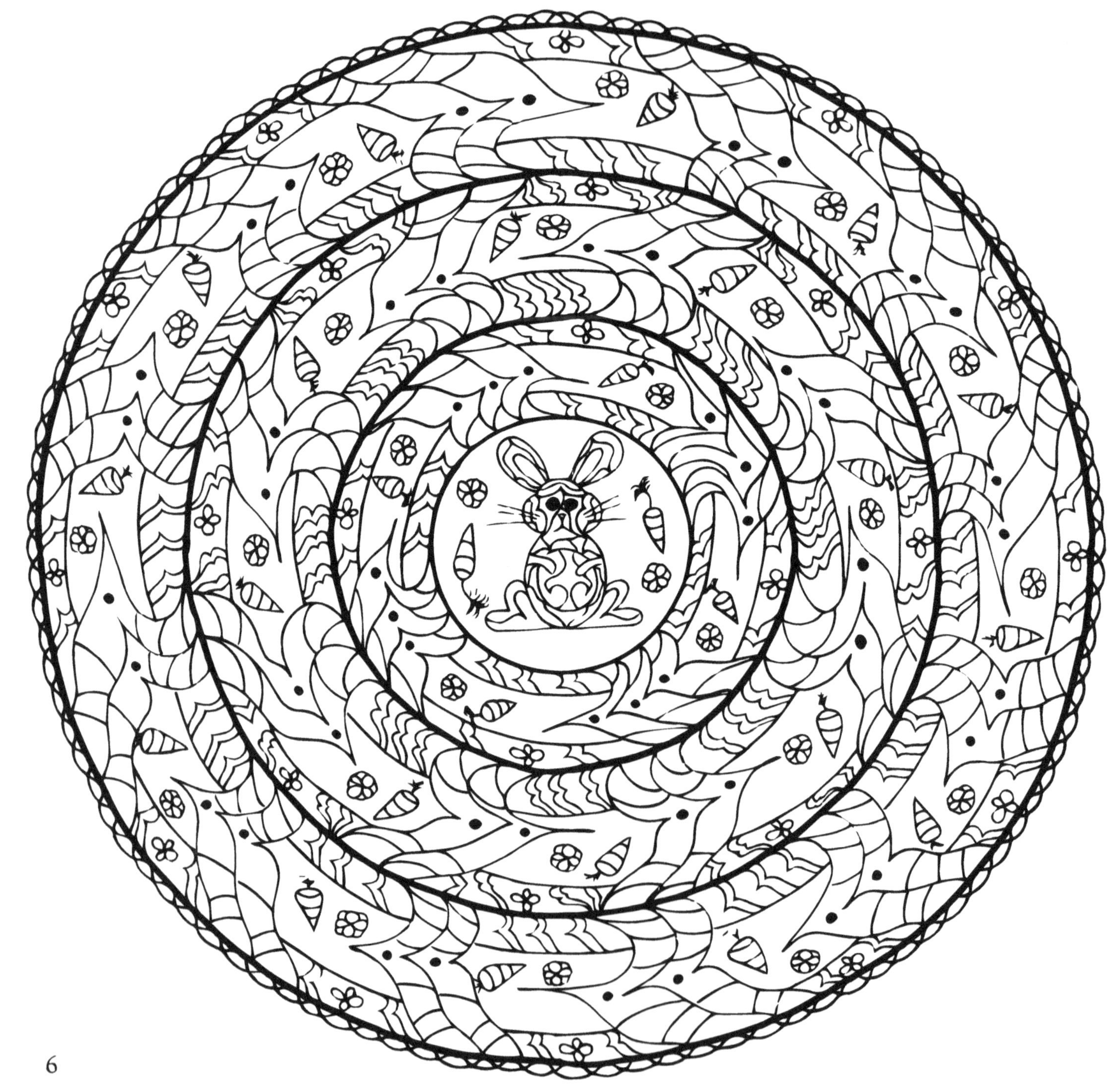

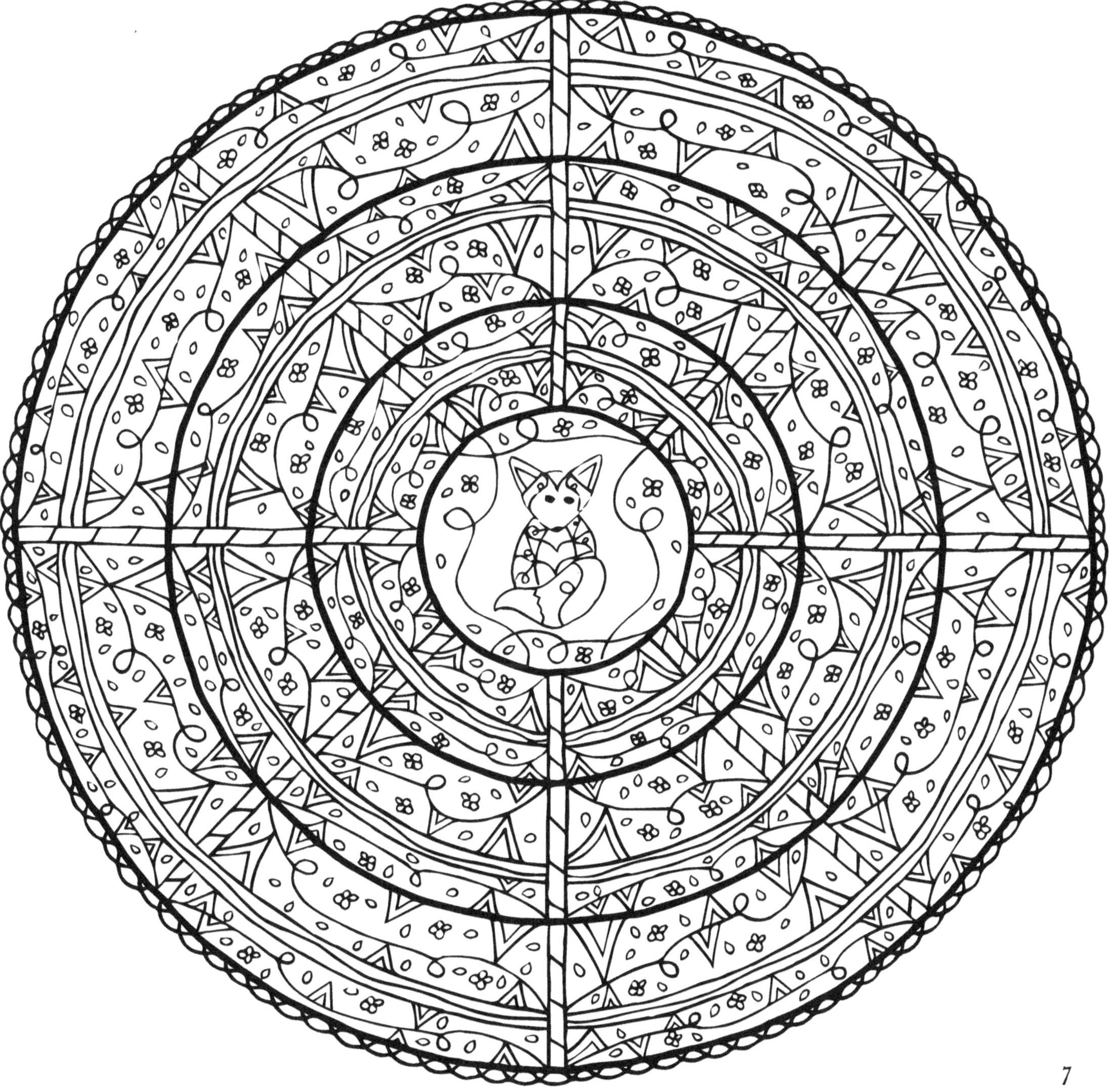

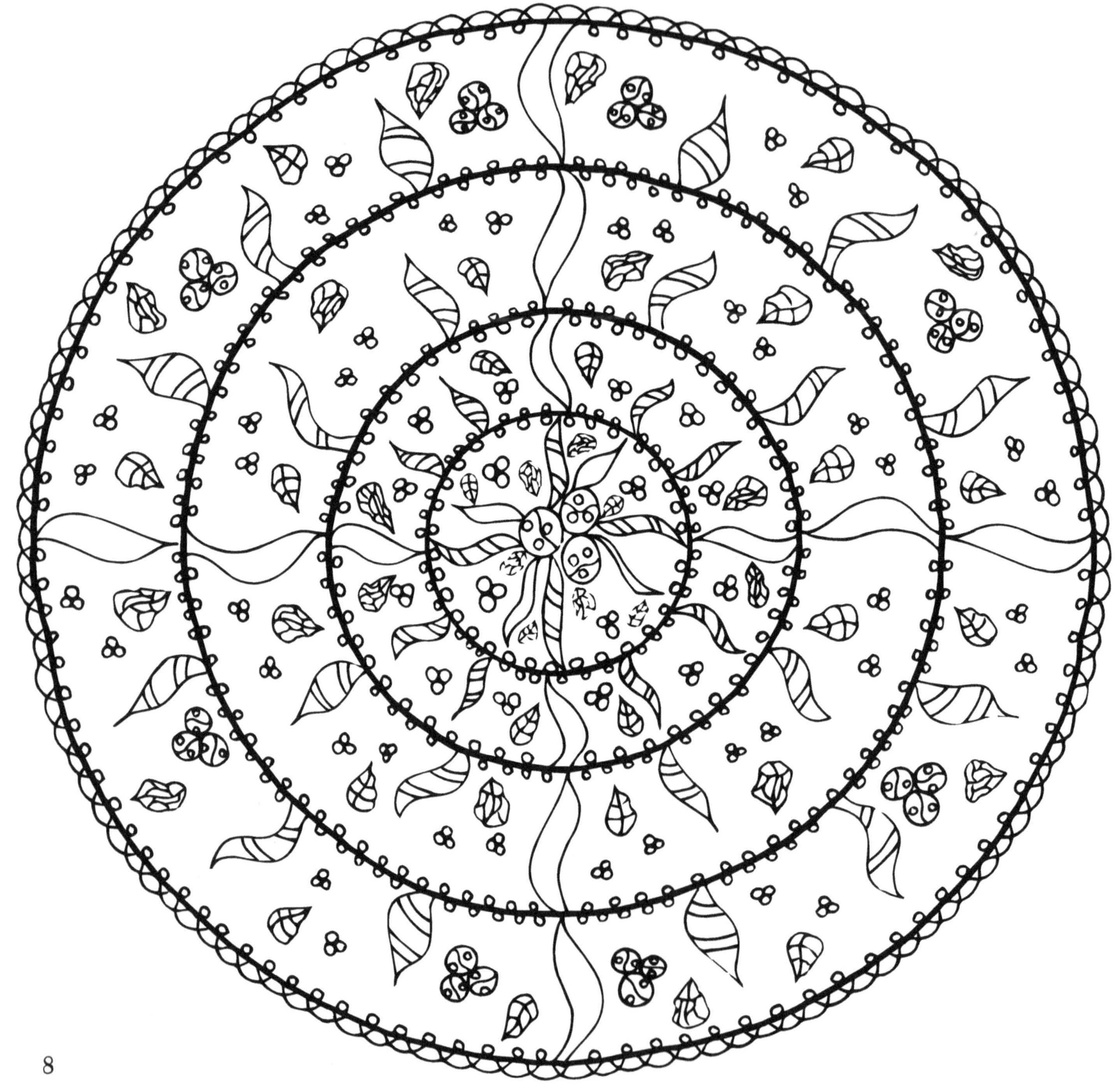

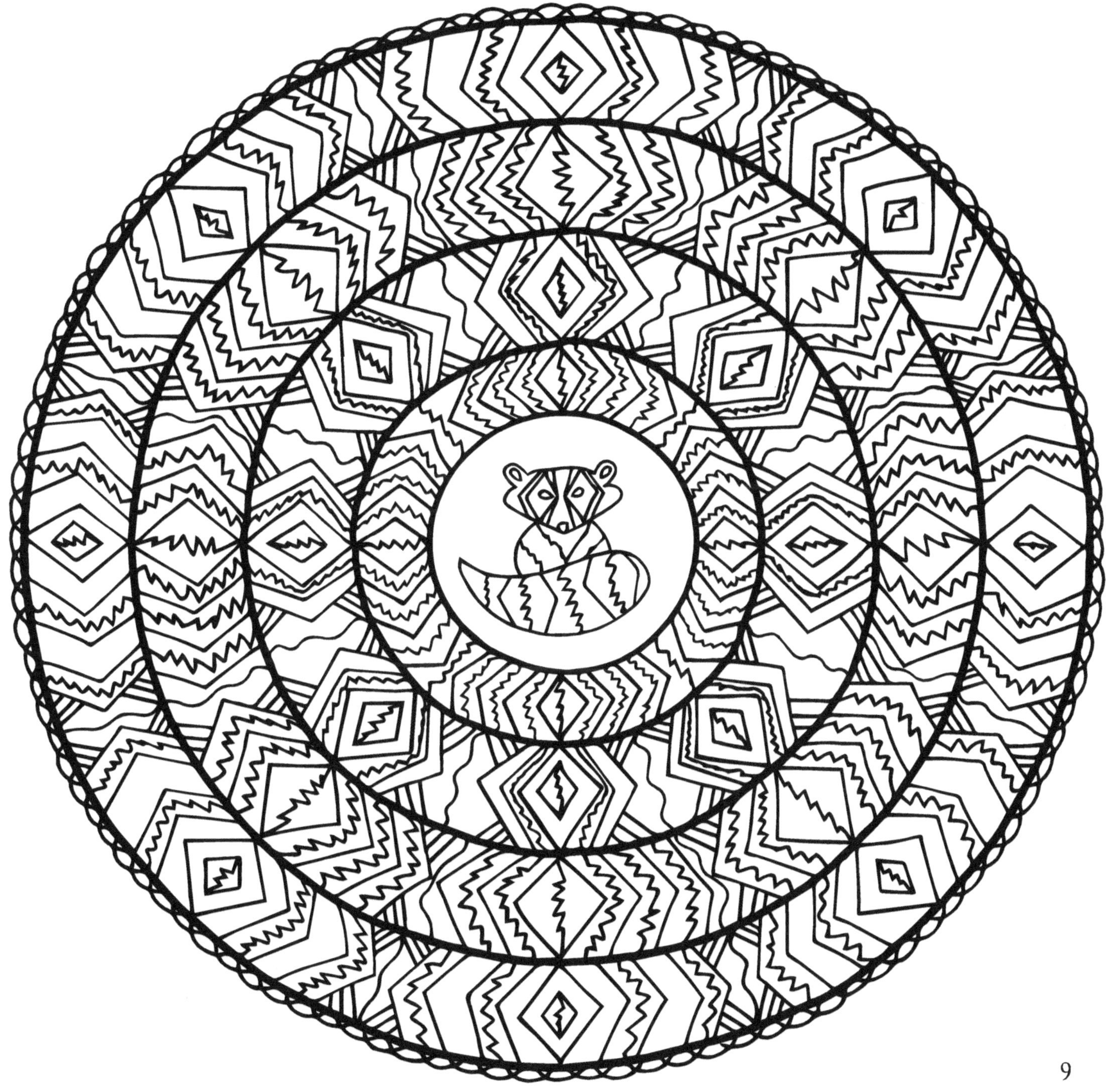

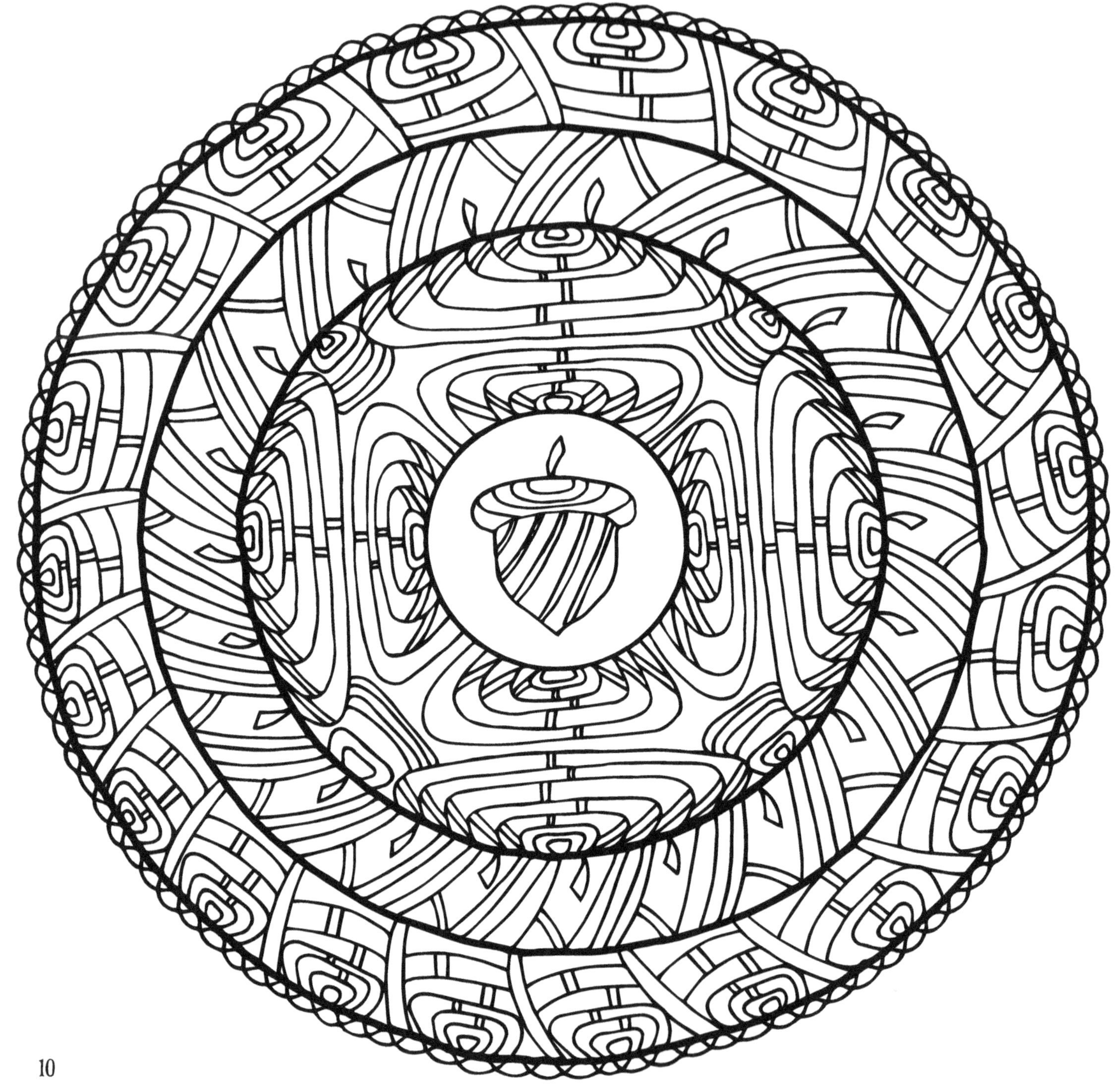

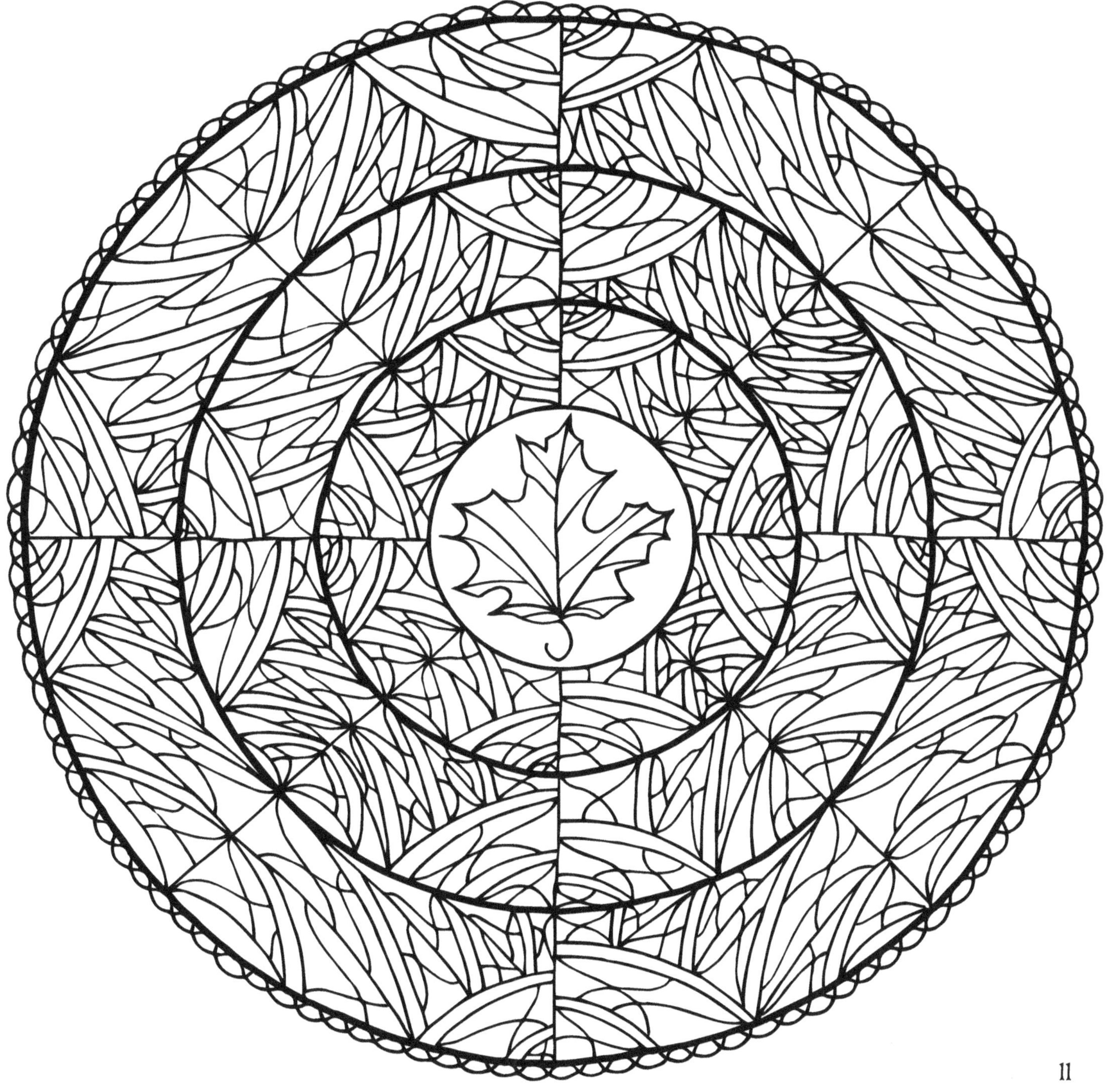

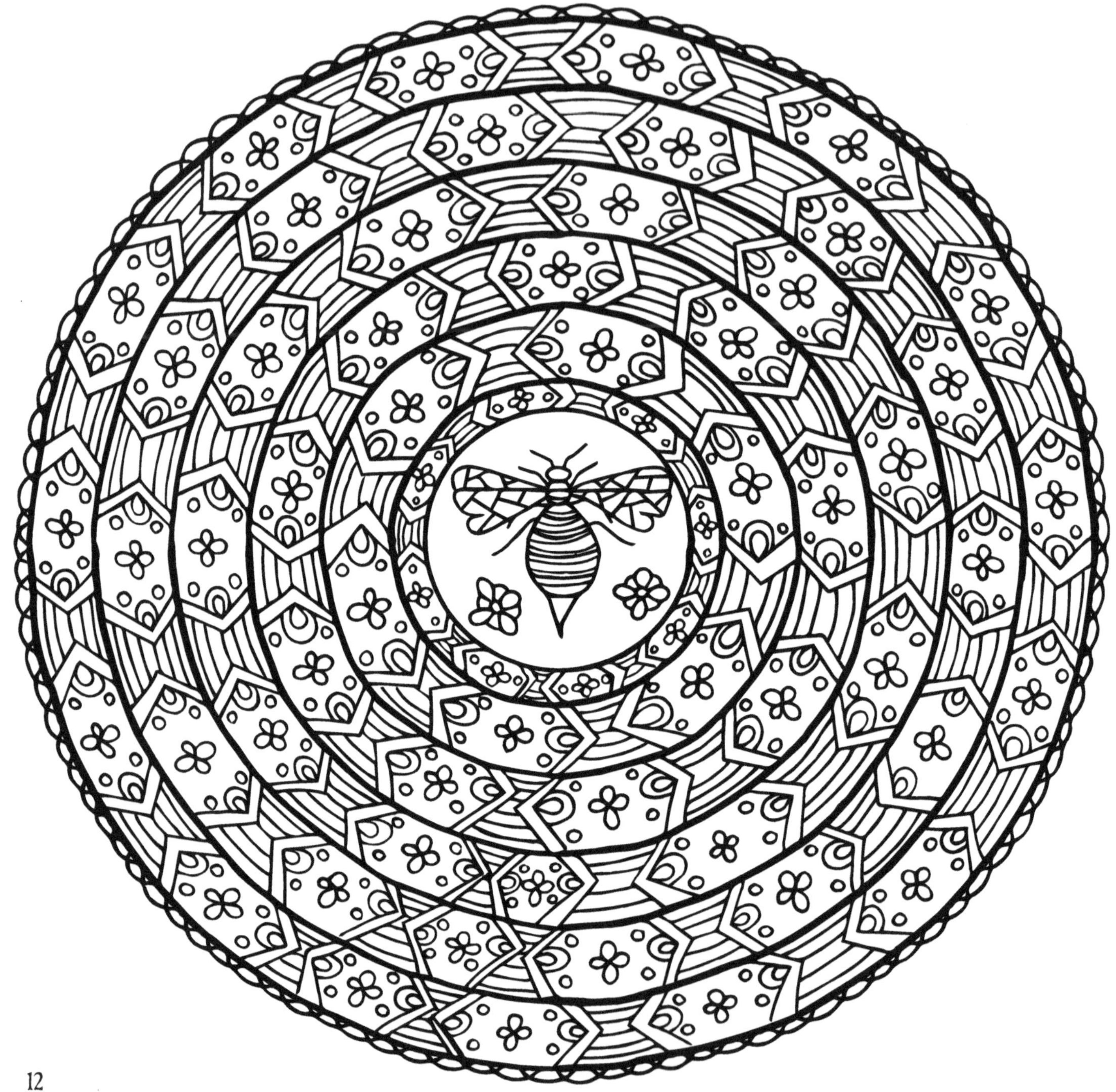

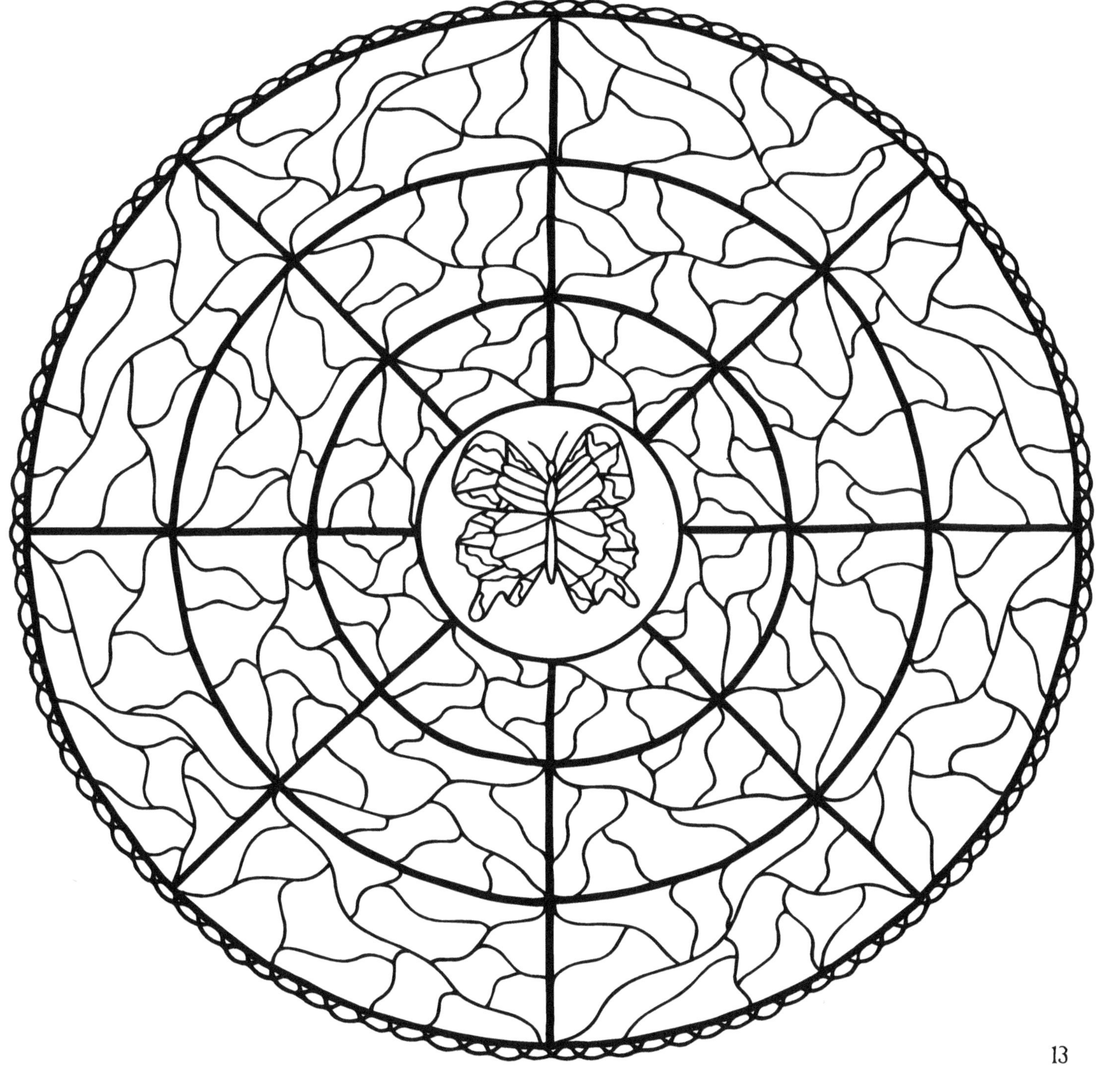

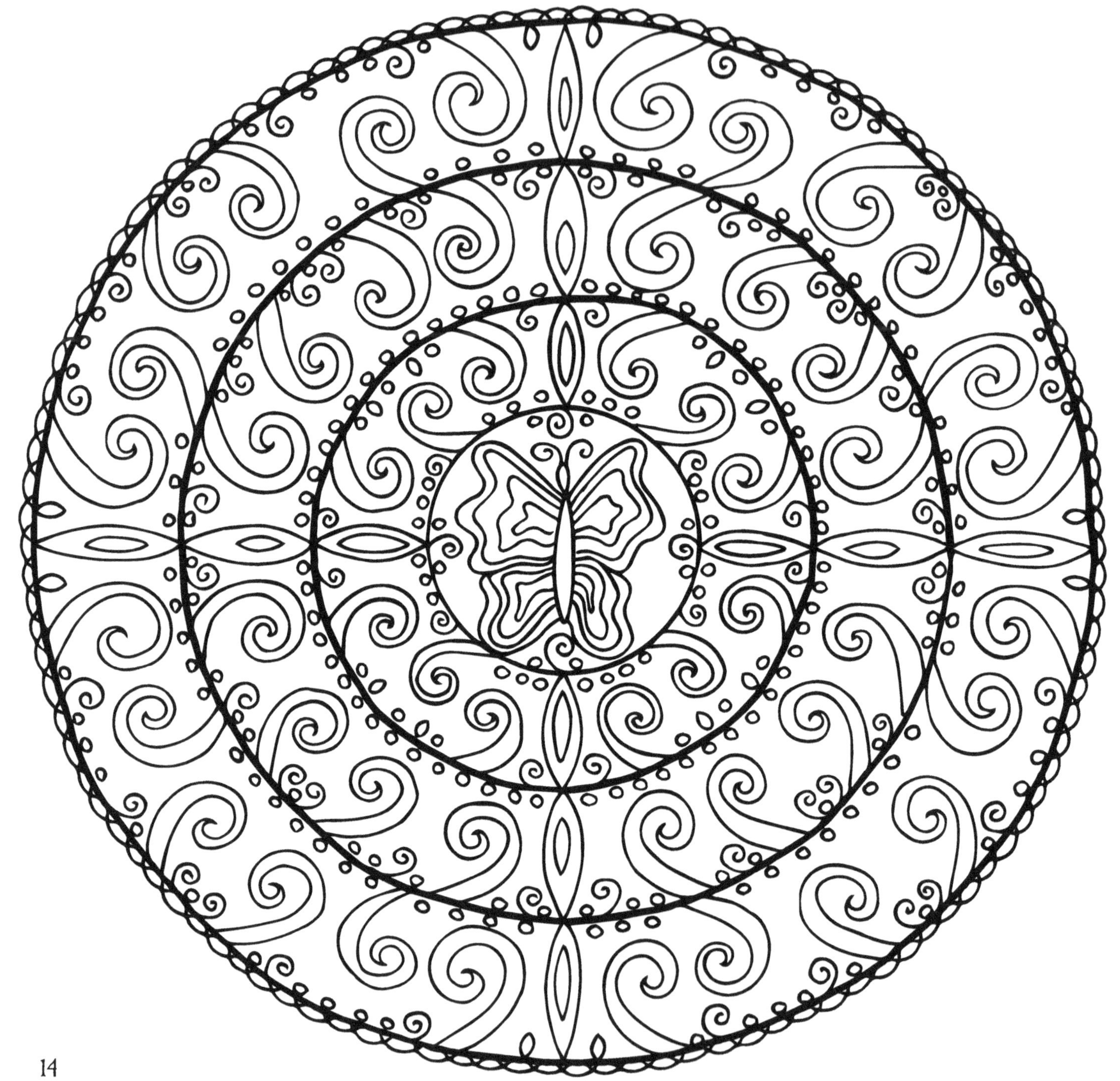

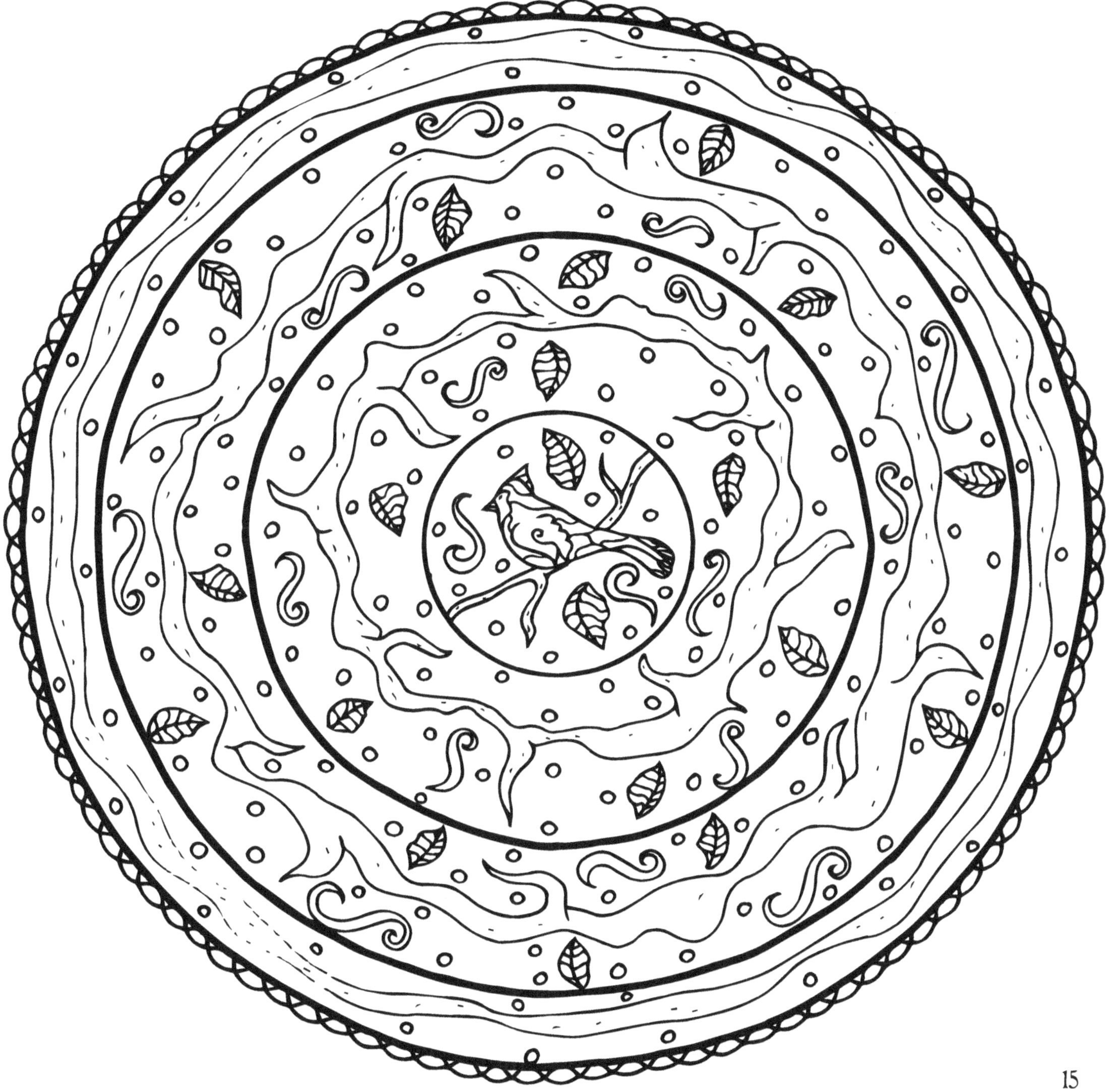

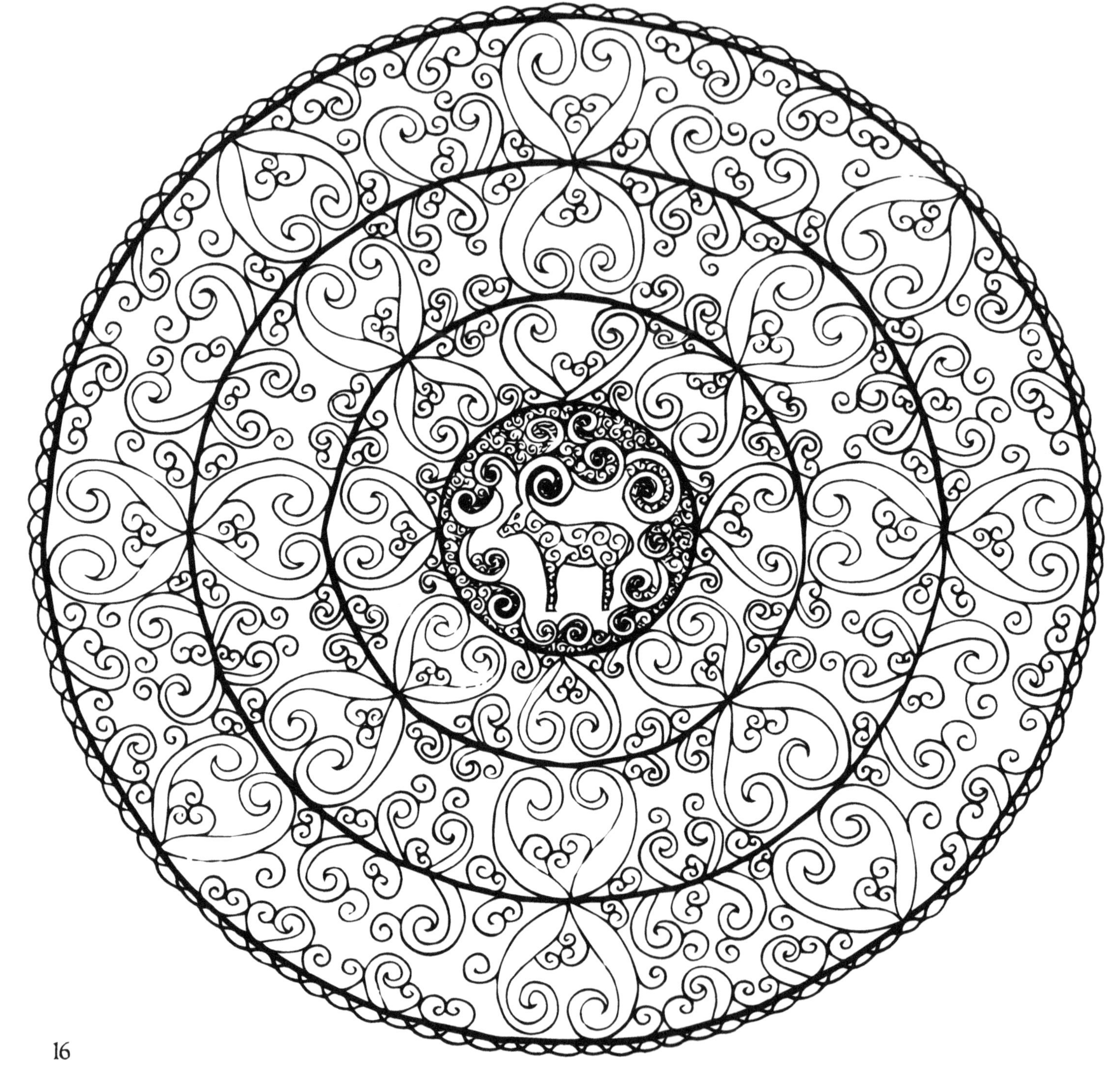

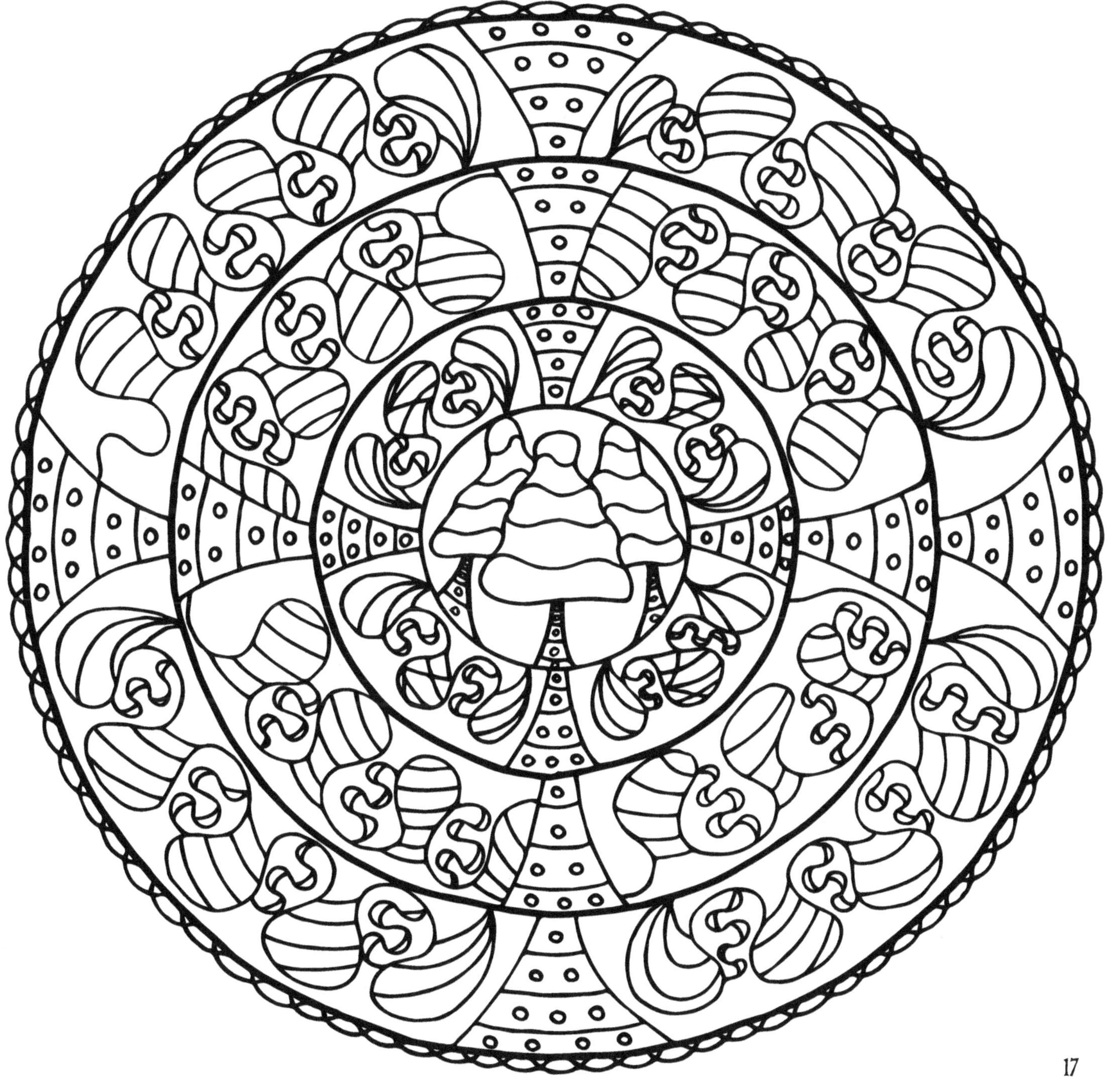

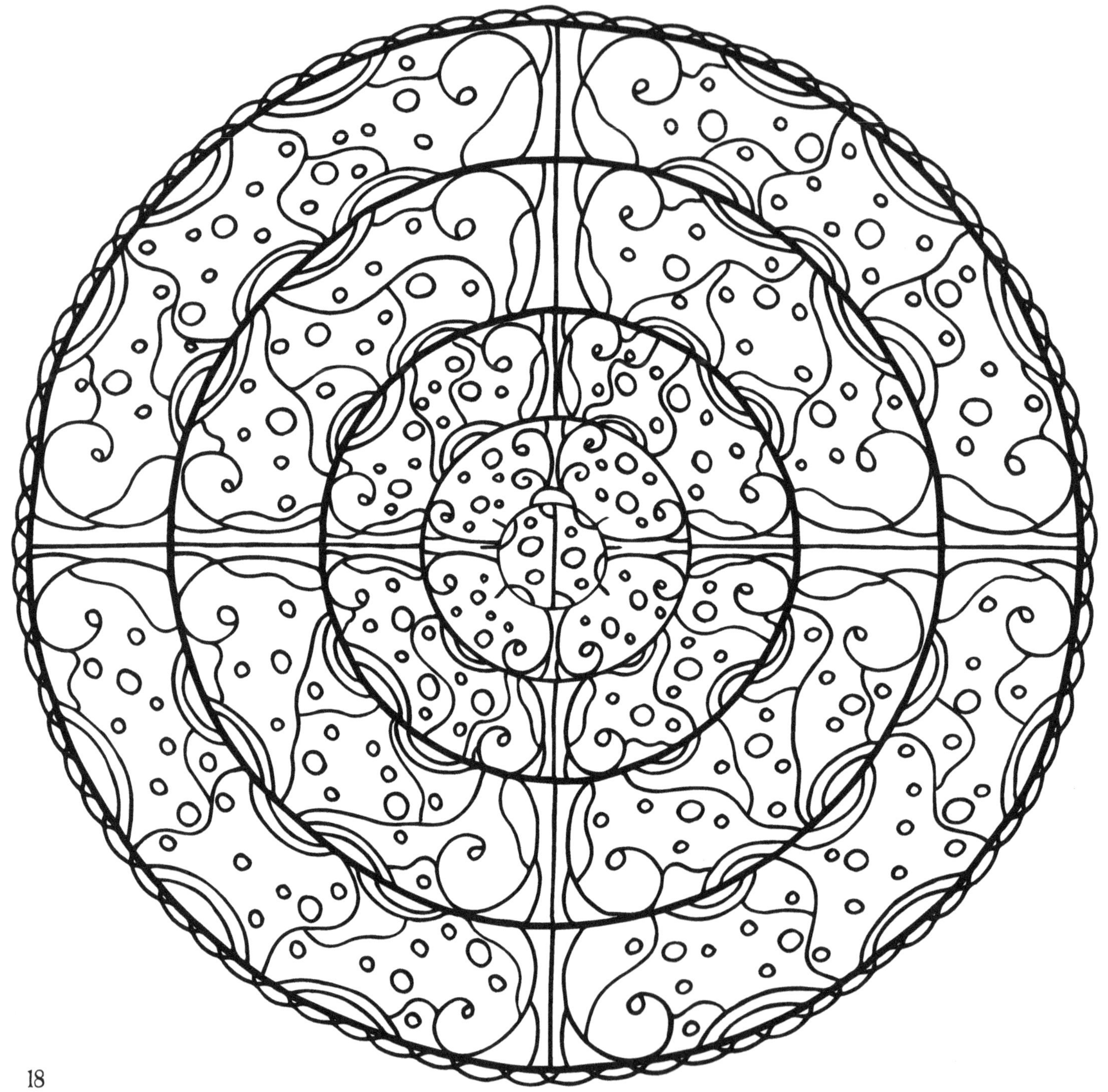

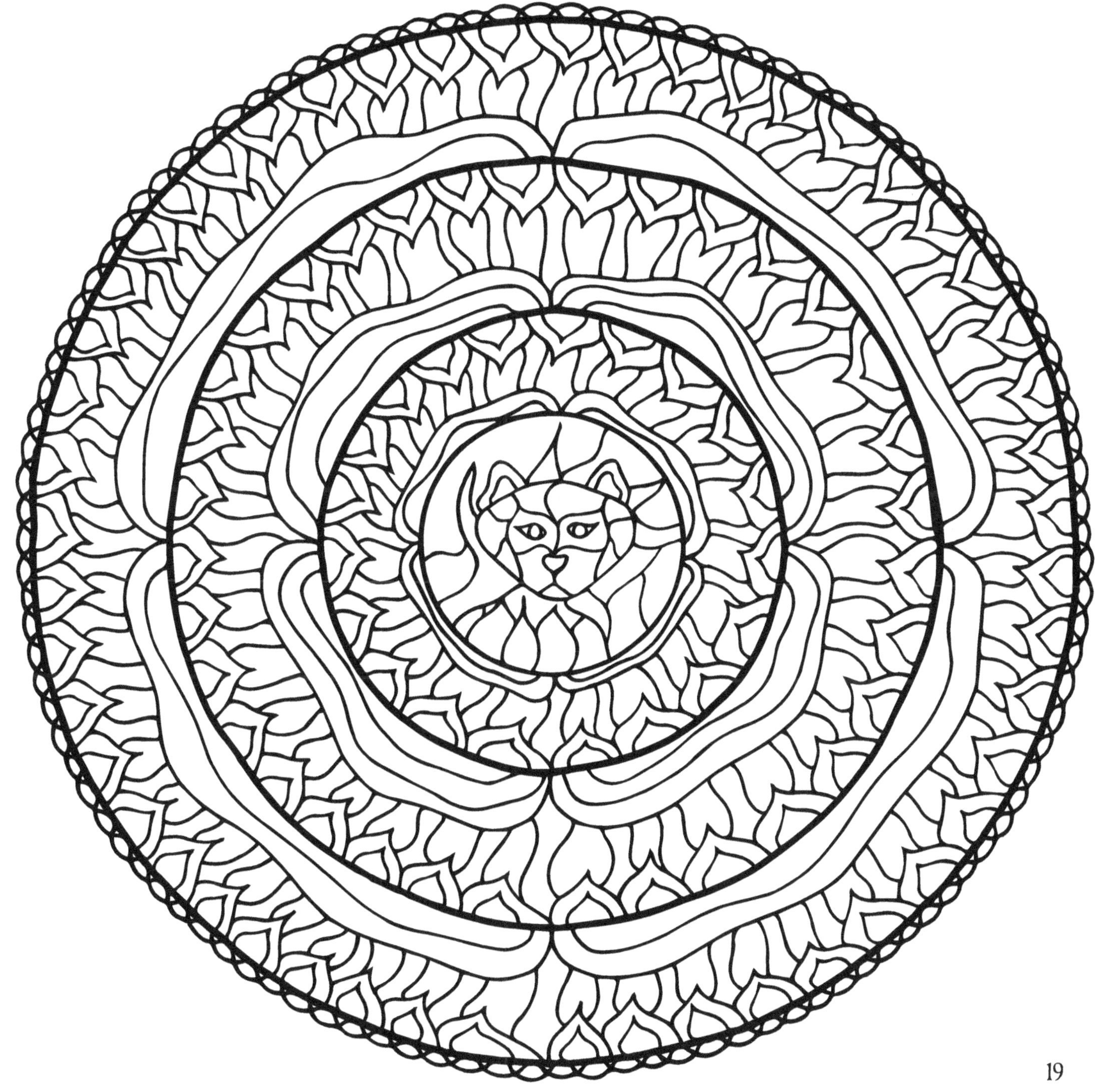

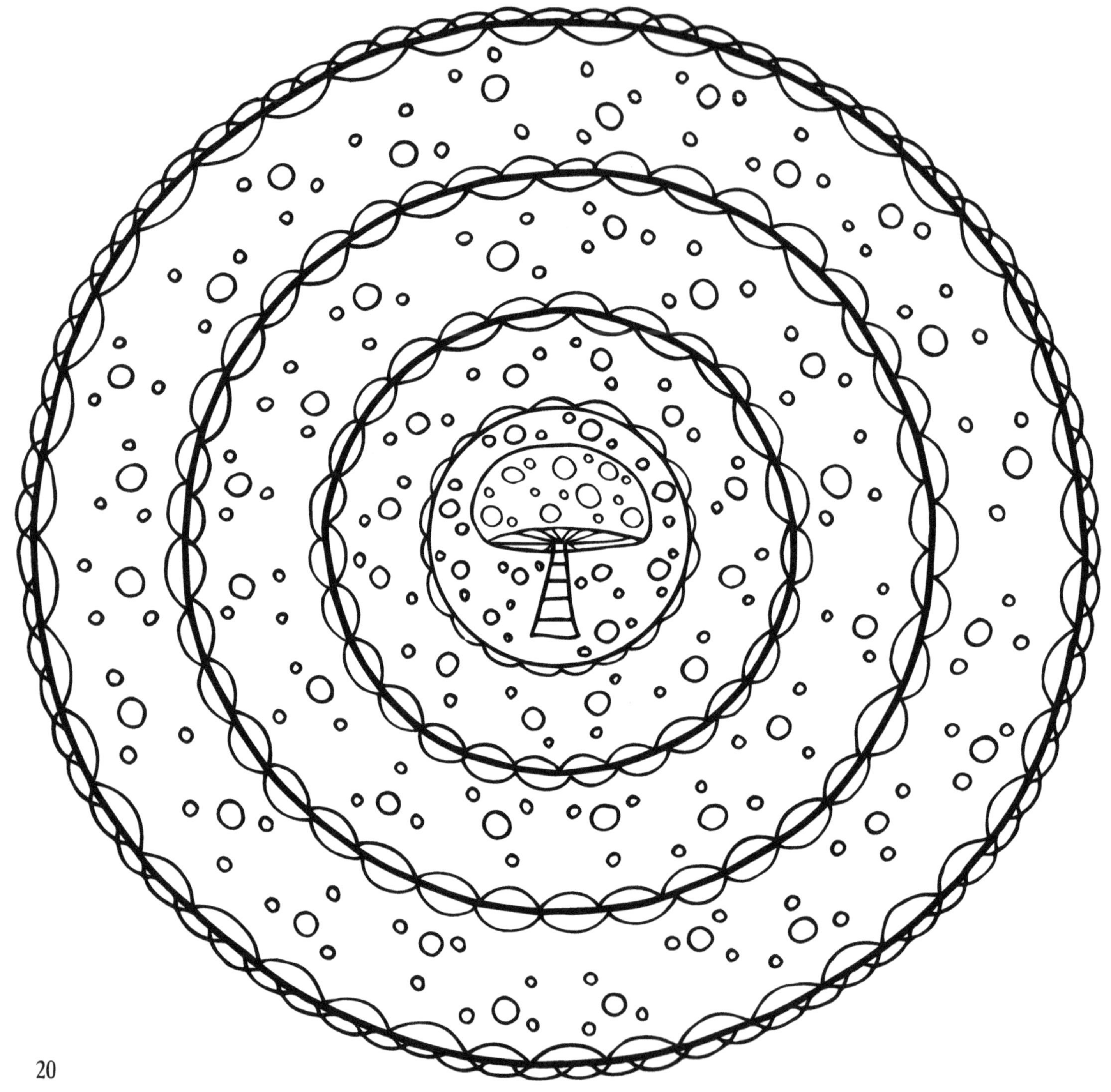

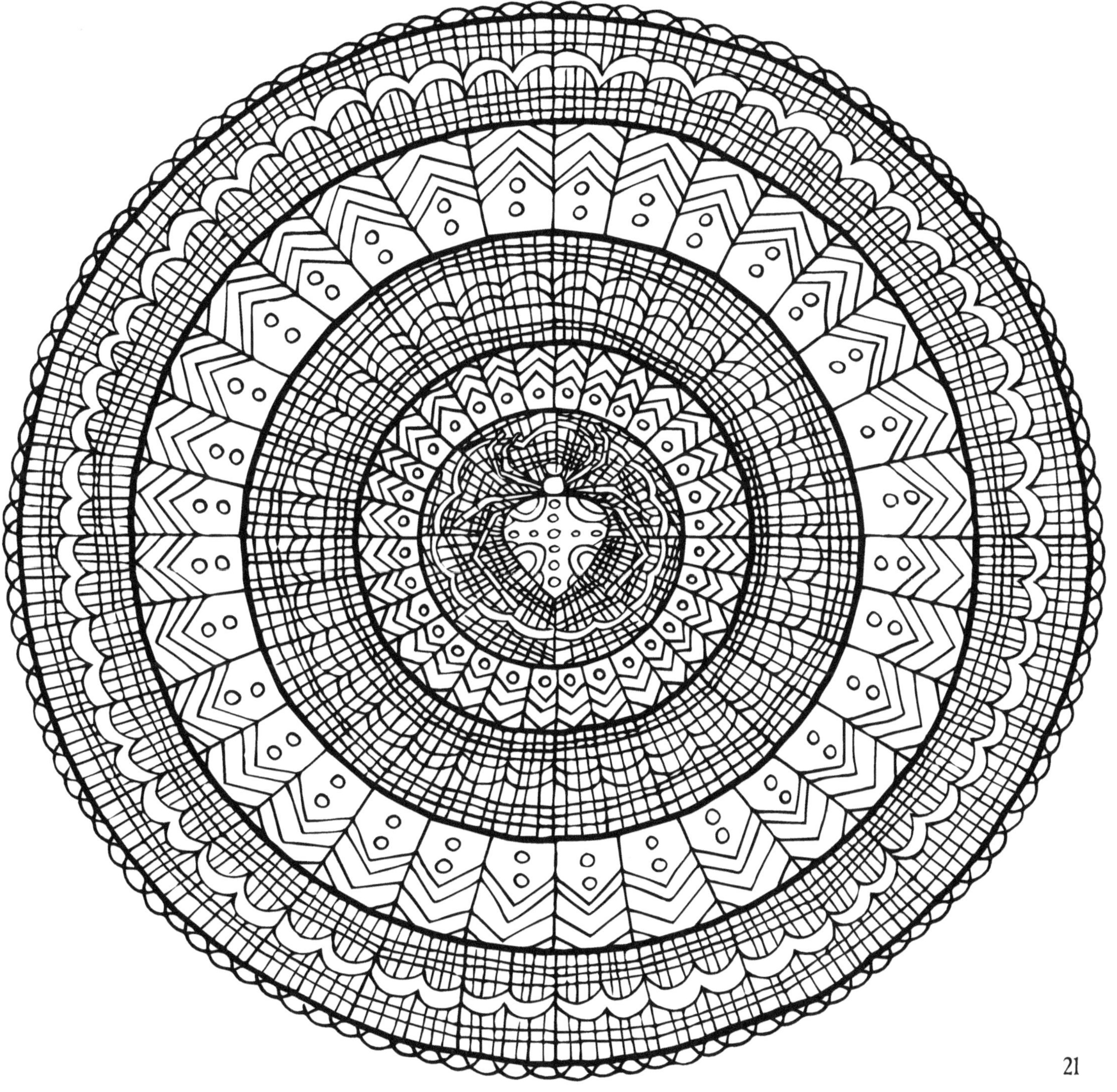

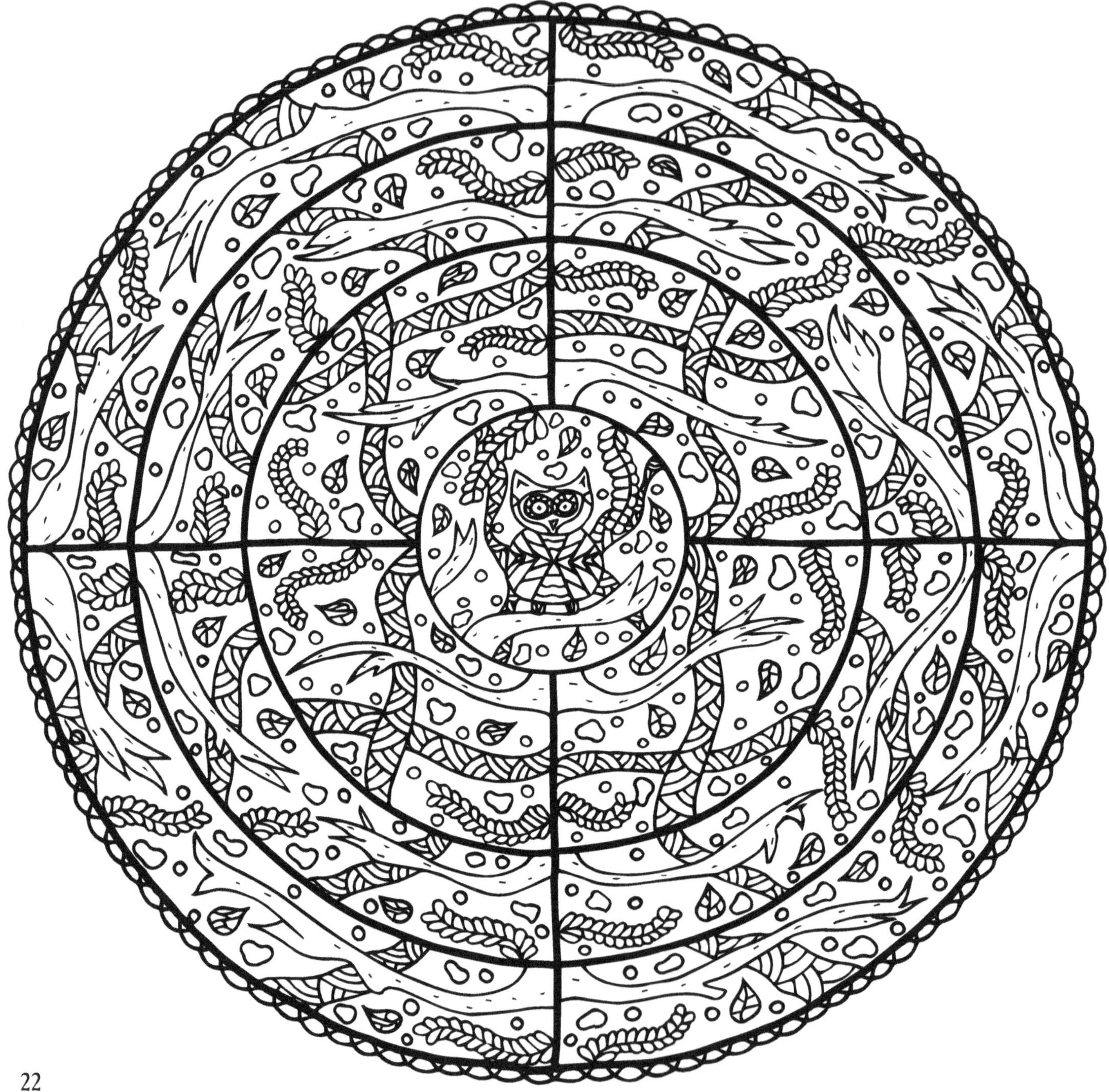

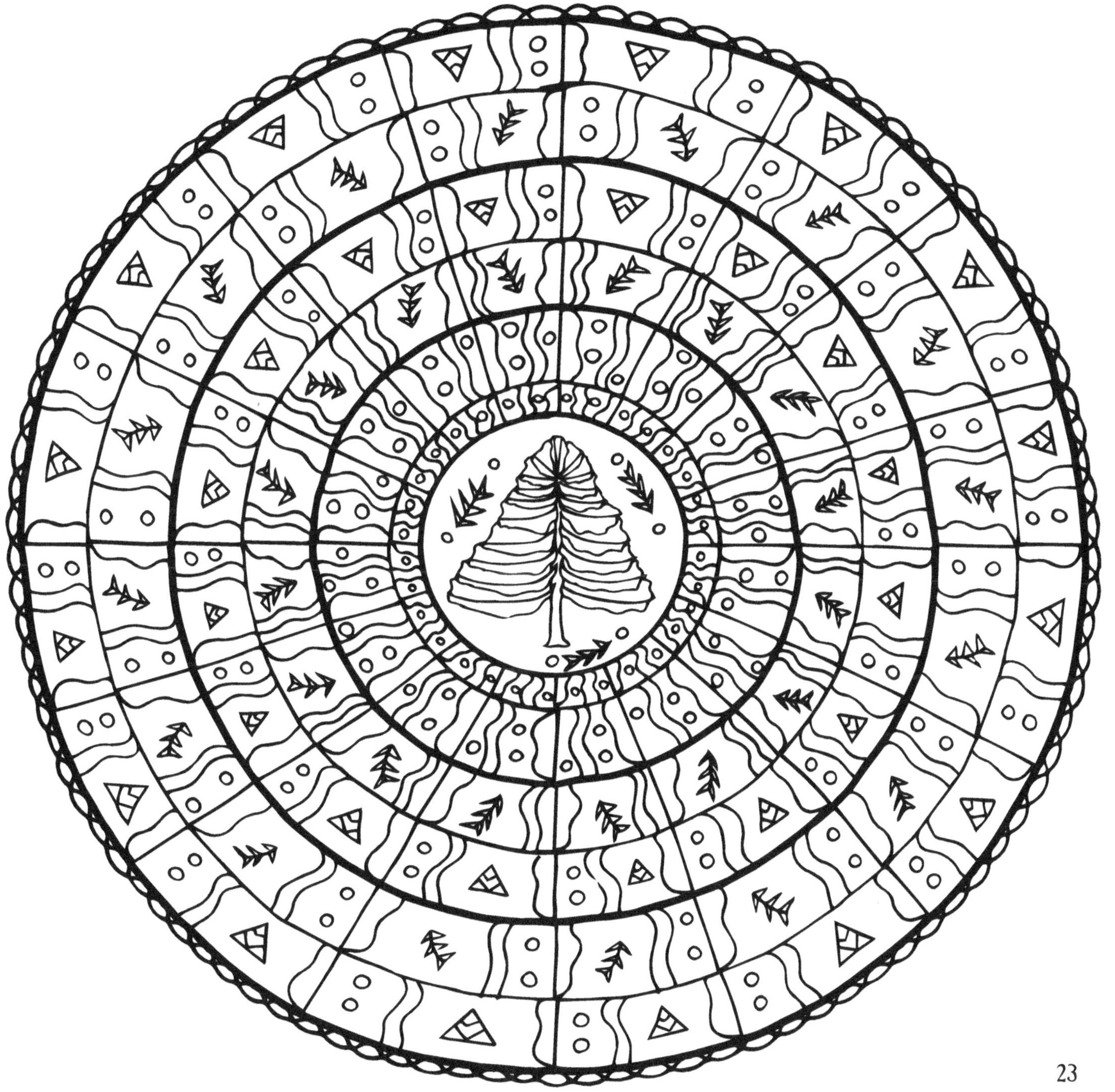

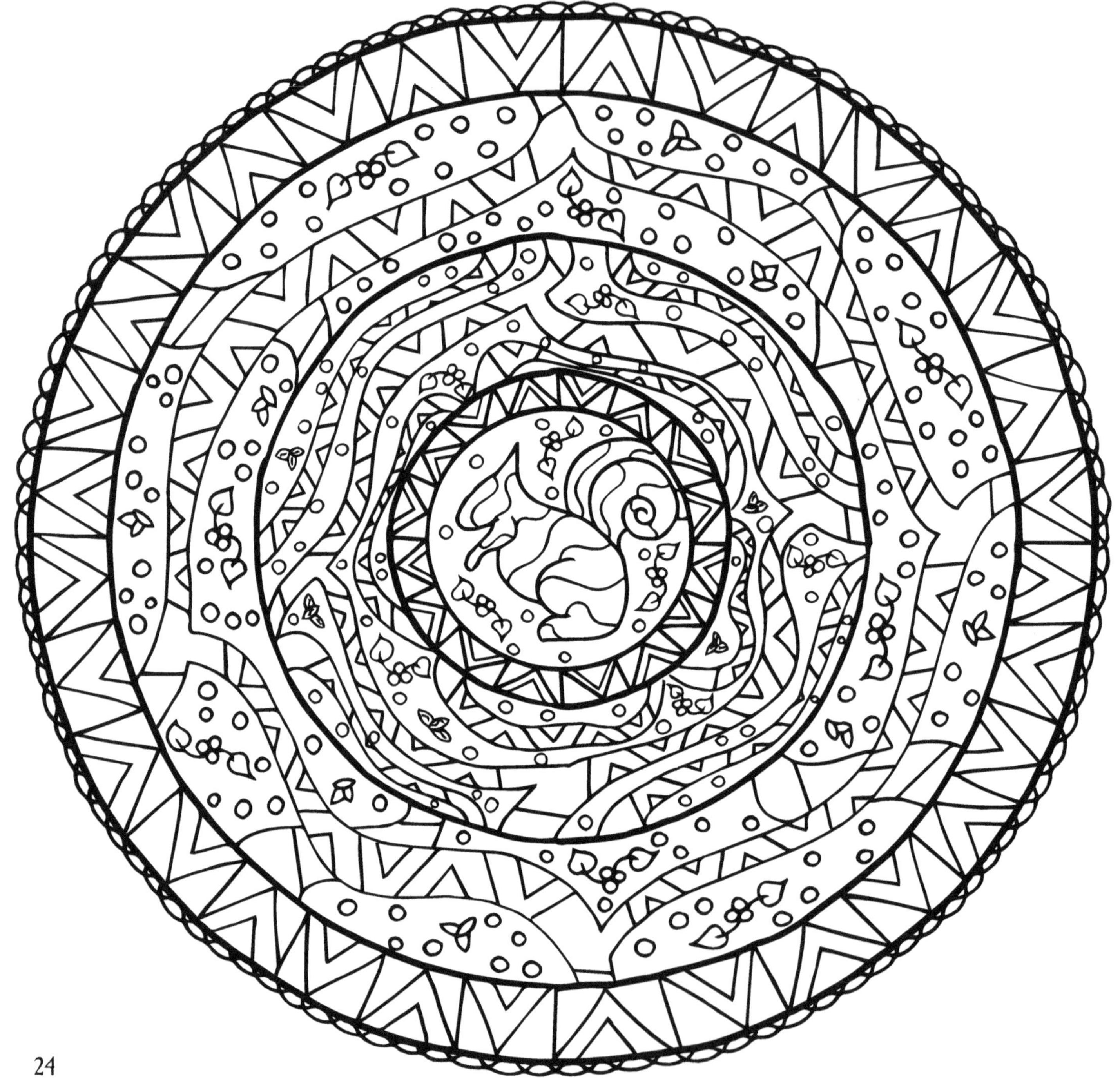

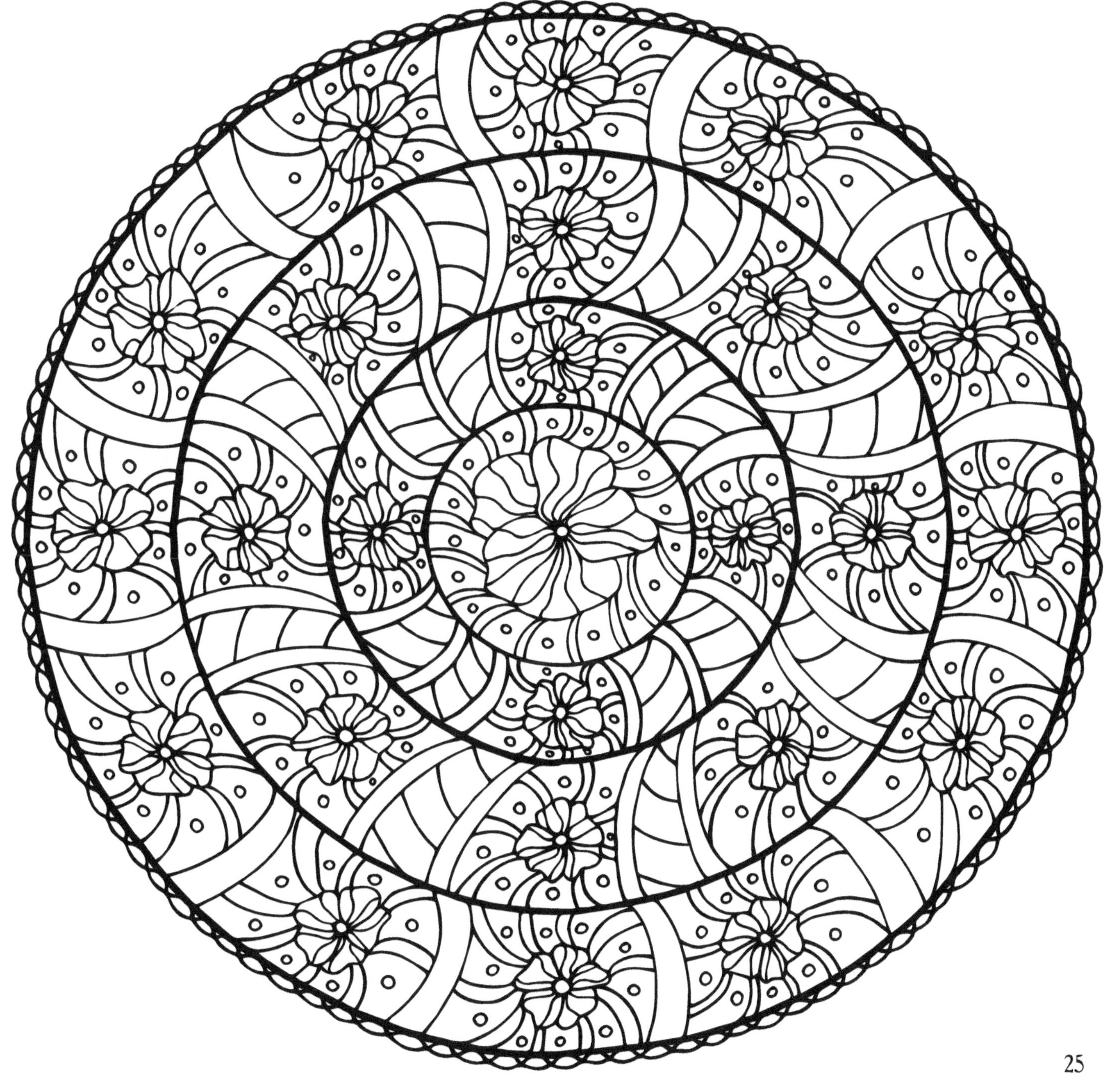

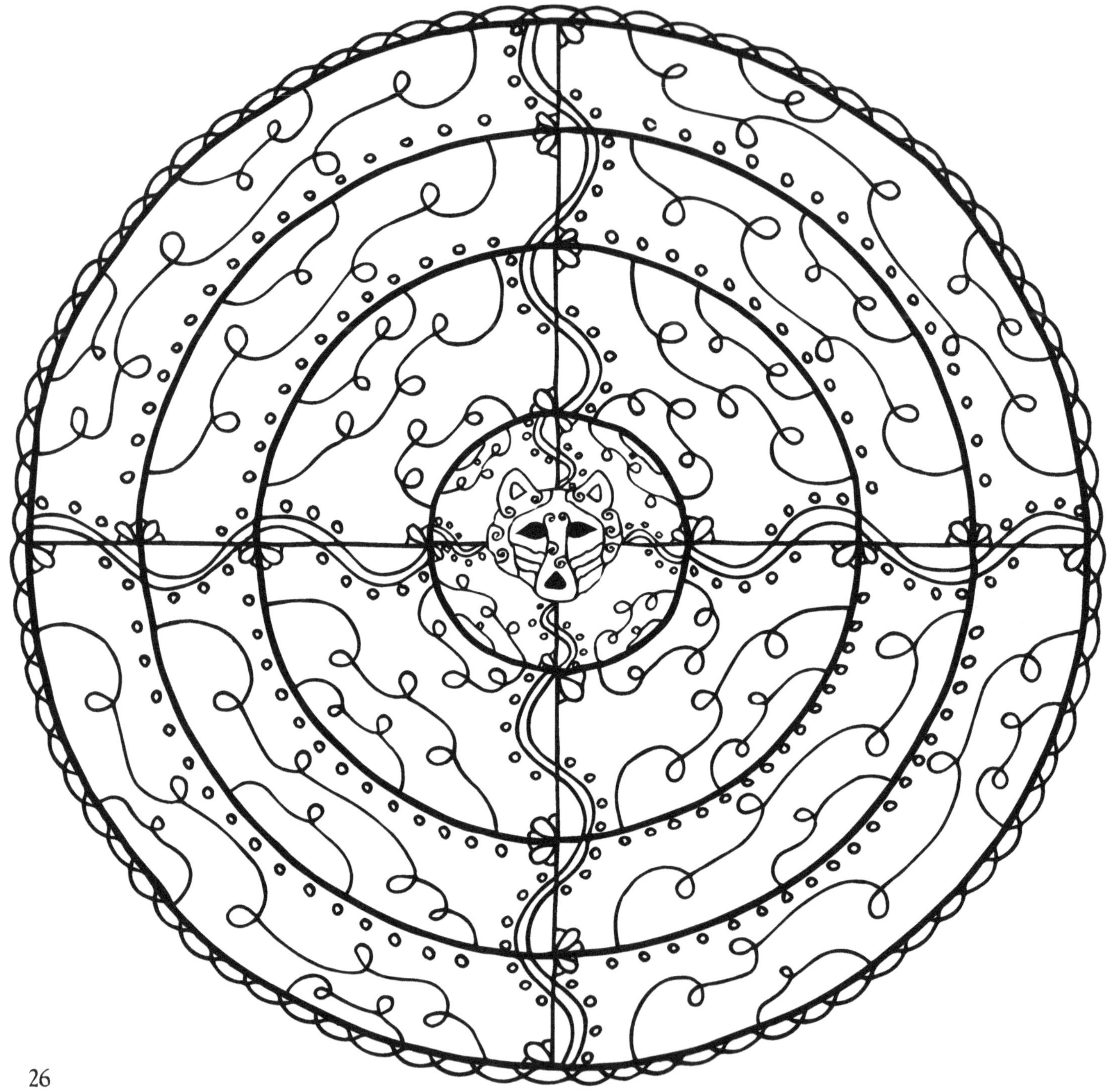

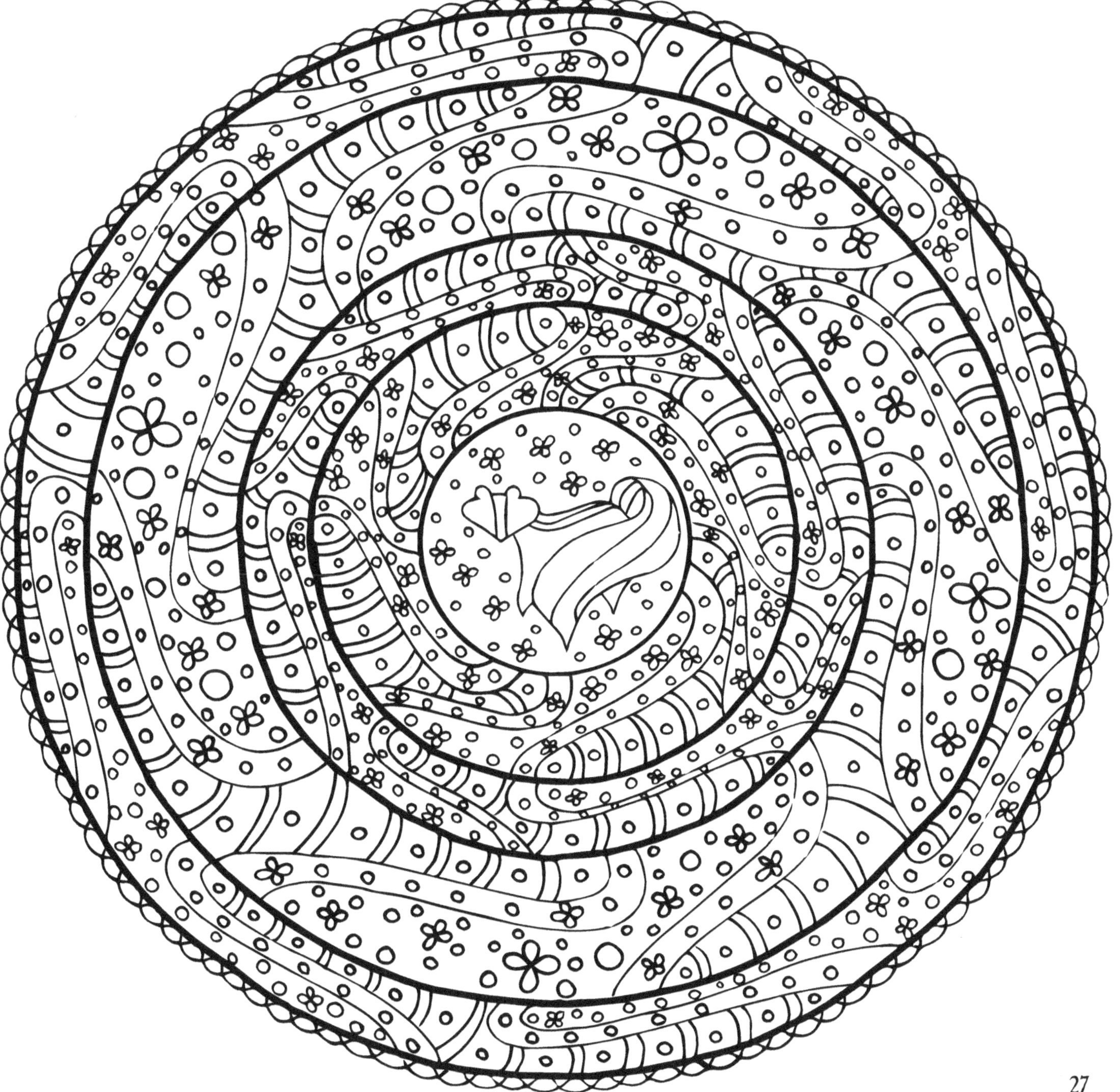

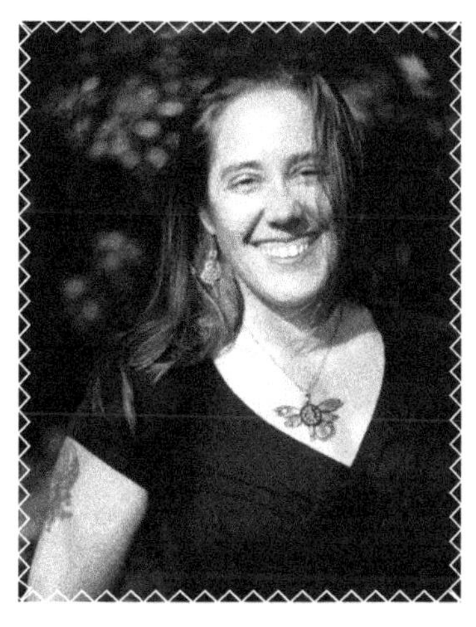

Rebecca is a self-proclaimed book nerd. In her spare time she doodles, then colors them in, and sells them under the catchy title of Fine Art Doodles. She also likes to practice calligraphy, make journals and stationery, take long hikes, and live in a perpetual mess of ongoing art projects. She lives in the stunning Southwest atop a beautiful mountain range with her husband and three loud children.

To see more of Rebecca's artwork and creations visit you can visit her website or her Etsy store:

www.Wordsremember.com
Etsy.com/Shop/Wordsremember